Summer Rain

Summer Rain

A Collection of Poems

Amina Mejdoubi

To my loving parents,
your support of my dreams has made
me the woman I am today.
To Laura Schneiders,
thank you for holding my hand in life
and while writing this book.

"The idea is to write it so that people hear it and it slides through the brain and goes to the heart."

-Maya Angelou

Contents

Dear reader,
I leave you with my heart
in your hands now.
Please take care of it.

*The bottom of each page has been intentionally left
blank for you! Your thoughts, your feelings and your
creativity after reading mine. Enjoy.

Cyclone

He gave me boy vibes
But you exuded manhood
With every move
Silly me!
I even loved the way your manly hands
showed off your veins as you sipped your coffee
I watched you gently touch the cookies with the top of your lips
and I wished for a second
I could be edible
too

Doubts pay me a visit
I find myself in a labyrinth of the same questions
Will he love me when I don't love myself
and can't see my worth?
Will he hold me down
when my heart drowns?

What happens after you fall in love?
Keep falling until you shatter your heart
to the point of unrecognition
or
Save yourself before it's too late

We tiptoed on our feelings
We pulled and pushed our hearts to safety
afraid of how we might eventually
destroy each other in the name of
Love

We dove into each other's secrets
so deeply
so quickly
so regrettably honest
and that
changed our narrative

I lovingly invited you into my heart
You didn't even take your shoes off
and walked all over it
like it was not
precious

All I ever wanted
was for your love to wrap
its arms around me
I wanted to know what kind of broken you are
in order to fix you in ways
I couldn't fix myself

I begged you to
tell me about what makes you
and breaks you
I begged you to
let me love you in ways I cannot name
I begged you to
Let me in and let me stay

I close my eyes so you can hold me closer
one more time
I linger in your imaginary presence
The smell in my sheets greets me
and reminds me that you are
no longer here
no longer mine…
I tried to fill your void
with someone else
who smelled different
and felt different
It wasn't a bad different
It just wasn't you

I never asked for all of you
yet you offered me your world
You spilled more of you onto me
and I enjoyed it
until my world merged into yours
and in a quick second
you realized that your heart was too shallow
for a love as deep as mine

I willingly stabbed my heart
when I believed the words out of your mouth
you
fucking
liar

You showed up at my door with a bouquet of red flags
I let you in
I vividly remember
wearing my big smile
that was later tarnished with tears of regret

I warned you that playing stupid games
will get you stupid prizes
but you insisted on becoming a champion
Congrats!

You felt cozy and smelled like home
You were once the deep breath
I couldn't take on my own
but just like home
we became strangers
and ended up all alone

You leashed my heart
and took it on a deceitful walk
Fuck you very much!

I am not amazing for you
but that's not the end of me
I poured my heart into yours
only for you to show me
that my heart deserves more than you could
ever give me

You teased my heart from a distance
It felt right
and I *almost* fell for your bullshit

You barged in on my heart
in a moment of stillness
and interrupted my feelings
You made yourself comfortable in my heart
without consent

You took my heart for granted
and I watched my love for you slowly fade away
like a burning fire eating through every emotion
my heart ever held for you

Foolish of me to think that you would ever
fall for my greatness
for you are used to sloppy seconds

Haunting memories of the past
Mind trips to the future
I am longing to become the girl I used to be again
Please take it easy on my heart
or
fucking
leave

I expected you to run a mile for me
but you couldn't even move an inch
of your pride to the side
to love me fairly
and I will always apologize to my heart
for the hurt you inflicted in me

You preyed on my vulnerability
and forced me to change
for a quick second
everything that made me who I am
to fit the description of
the woman you desired

My stiff body language gave away
the answer to how I felt around you
Your smile forced itself upon me
and I stood there
lifeless

You made me feel
unwanted
undesired
small
and I made sure
you felt the opposite of that
It's a shame that I chose you
over myself

Your love was a plague
that took over my heart
infested my thoughts
and scarred my soul

You lured my heart
and served me leftover feelings
on a platter of gold

I hope you felt like the man you are not
after spreading me thin with your sweet lies
to portray someone far from who you are
You are what I fear in a man
and loving me was never your plan

You pushed my tender areas
and made my wounds bleed again
You left and cowardly watched me from afar
bandage myself back to sanity

I forced myself to sleep
every time you pinned your body against mine
tears spreading their arms to embrace me
with every stroke
that felt like a stab to my womanhood

You are one of the many thoughts
that come rushing to the surface
in a moment of quiet
truth and uncertainty
to vehemently deny
the peace of mind
that took long nights
for me to find

You ruptured every womanly dream in me
before my eyes
You stole many firsts from me
You skinned me alive and threw me
to the wolves

It truly shattered my heart
that you loved me to pieces
and left my heart in puzzled pieces
I couldn't manage to put back together

I peeled layers of myself in the comfort of your jokes
You judged me
left me there
drowning in shame
Did that make you feel more like a man?

I allowed you to disrespect my heart
and feed me lies
I allowed myself to rot in your presence
until I no longer existed
neither in your world
nor mine

I draped my feelings on your heart
like a dirty garment forgotten on a chair
fighting for your attention in despair
I knew you would never be mine
but I chose to lie to myself for the sake of time
for our lust was only part-time

I overdid everything including
loving you
You resisted my love every way I served it to you
I wanted you to want me
but your indifference silently
killed me
I made a man of you
and in return
you insulted
every fiber of womanhood in me

I should have allowed the hands of loneliness to get me
rather than end up in your cold arms
that left an icy imprint on my heart
which took years of self-love to melt

Your actions showed me
that you wouldn't be around for a while
so I penciled your name in my book of life

You loved the sense out of my mind
I blindly followed your desires
and ignored the cries of mine
so tonight
I light this candle as a tribute
to the dreams I left behind
I am sorry I lost my battle
for you in the name of love

You played hangman with your words
and ended up killing yourself
in
MY
story

You ran back to me to stroke your ego
E. V. E. R. Y. T. I. M. E
you acted less than the man you always claimed to be
I let you back in my heart
E. V. E. R. Y. T. I. M. E
until I realized that loving you
was slowly killing me

Every season
you gave me a different reason
to leave you
but I stayed to prove my heart wrong

I couldn't hate you
at least for the time you pretended to love me
when the sun flaunted its rays on us
and I spilled my brown skin onto yours
in the middle of that hot summer Friday

You loved me privately
and played me in public
and that will never
sit well
with
the scorpio woman
in me

You were a nightmare
a bullet
I dodged with my eyes closed

I clearly saw the lies firing from your mouth
but I chose not to make eye contact with them for too long
I lied to myself instead
to keep myself safe from any more
heartache

You weighed my chest down
and squeezed my love for you out of it
I let you get away with it
I set my pride aside
for a last stupid chance of love

Eyes talk
and
yours blatantly lied to me

You left an earth-shattering pain on my chest
every time I couldn't find a reason
to defend why you left
abruptly like a thunder on a summer night
without any warning
or a sign

My bulletproof heart
still got burned by your bullet shells
when I got too close to you

You are a human stain
I can't get off my new clean-slated life
a nightmare that keeps revisiting me
in broad daylight

Your words hit me like waves
in a large sea of lies
bouncing me back and forth
lifeless
I drowned myself
while the whole world was watching

I held on to hope
to keep you around longer
lie to myself further
and fall for you deeper
hoping that my love for you
would make you linger

After every failed love story
my mind ran back to your heart
for safety
to wonder where we would be
if you had not given up on us

He said:
"You are an amazing, strong, bold,
brave, fun, unique, talented, beautiful, driven,
adventurous, resilient, soft soldier of a woman and
your presence in my life for this short time has been a treasure.
You have a friend and a confidant in me."
and I never saw him again...

Your occasional hello is a cry for help
and we both know that
but my heart is no longer your refuge
whenever you feel displaced
by other women

I heard it poured sadness on your heart again
Is this why you ran to mine for shelter?
You are no longer welcome back in
to this heart you willingly left
to find strength on its own

His heart breaks
when his memory wakes
He runs to me for words of comfort
in his most hopeless state

I wondered if I will ever become my whole self again
without your presence
without your touch
without your breath whispering poems in my ear
but look at me now
rhyming about the hurt you
gifted me

You ruined me
just enough
to shake me up
and wake me up
from my hopeless romantic ways
that led me to your poisonous arms

Hands to heart comforting my hesitant shaky voice
Life flashed before my eyes
when we stood there breathless
to say our goodbyes

All the cards are stacked beautifully
yet no feeling in sight
you are far from what I want
so move on to the next heart
to someone who can
better see your light

What keeps bringing you back to my cold arms
that feel unwelcoming and uninviting
to your lazy love?
You make me feel small
and less than the woman I am
even in the way you say my name

We won't last
You are safe
You are water
I am the fire missing within you
and I am not willing to save you

You were a bridge of emotions I used to cross
to the other side of my pain
and for that
I am sincerely sorry

My teardrops stained my diary
as my pen bled through the paper
when I saw a man cry tears of manhood
from losing his heart to me

You were the greatest reminder
that not every male is a man
not every promise is kept
and not every word is meant

My love is not for bargain
feel free to leave

I will burn your promises
with the fire of your lies
I will sprinkle your ashes of love
in a deep sea of grief
to forget that your fingers
ever ran across my body

My reserve of love is empty
from watering the wrong souls
I hope someone notices mine
before it completely dries

I am free of your monstrous words
but lost within myself
You ripped apart my dignity
with your bare hands
in the name of love

I trusted you enough
to stitch me back together
but I soon realized that
I am the only person
whose thread is thick enough
to patch me back to happiness

Do you think my heart is stupid enough
to want you back again
after leaving it stranded
in the middle of the journey
we both started?

I deserve more than the crumbs of love
I allowed you to serve me
over and over again

My heart feels heavy
yet light
I had to let you go
knowing that I still jump from happiness
every time I hear your name

I loved you in ways I didn't know possible
and I hated myself all along for doing it
so thanks for a lesson in self-love
and inner healing

They picked my rose and left me thorns
Worry not
my heart
for you are a rose
that's always destined to bloom

While everyone slept
I drew an image of us
and what life would have been
if you had kept your promises
and never spit on my love for you

You miss my love
and I can clearly see it
in your forced smile
in your late-night messages
and definitely
in all the women after me

I knew we had reached a dead end
when I stopped coming up
with excuses for you
every time you cut my heart open
with promises that were
too heavy for you to carry

Our ending was beautifully tragic
in every ruinous way there is
in the books of forbidden love

As much as I love you
I love myself more
So I let you go back
to yourself where
I don't belong anymore

Like we never happened
we were a blur of unnecessary emotions
A cursed love story
without a climax

I never thought I was turn you into poetry
'cause poetry is for sad lovers
and you made my heart smile
a real genuine smile
but look at me now
you are nothing but
a sad poem to me

And just like that
they leave like they were never here
like they never loved every detail about us
like they never tickled our heart strings
like they never ever loved us

I heard you miss my loud laughter
my stupid jokes
and my full-of-life presence
to fill up your
empty
pathetic
and vacant
world

People don't change
They just get too comfortable
and reveal layers of themselves
they never intended for us to see

I set myself free from you
and I found myself
like a fresh pot of morning coffee
ready to be savored and loved
by the right heart

Heatwave

Get comfortable
make my heart your home
and let me show you
how beautiful it is
inside my soul

I am a madwoman
chasing happiness in temporary
places and faces
to stay sane
Please don't judge me
as I navigate this world
of heartbreak
all alone

My heart is swollen
heavy and spent
from being repeatedly poked in its raw wounds
by different people
in the name of love

My heart is burdened with fake promises
ill-intentioned
half-assed people
and everything that weighs it down

Late at night
I talk to my sorrows
and wonder how many times
in this lifetime
I lost meaningful words
at the hands of silence and pride
and how many conversations
slowly died in the arms of regret

Sometimes I can't allow myself to feel
for I will quickly crumble apart
and never be able to heal

A public apology to my younger self:
I am sorry I didn't know any better
I am really sorry
I didn't protect you
I didn't stand up for you
I didn't love you
I didn't listen to you
I didn't take care of you
I am sorry I allowed people to take advantage of you
I am sorry I let you love the wrong people
I am sorry you felt like you didn't have a voice or a choice
I am sorry you had to go through all of that to become the woman you are today

My heart forcibly walks me through a labyrinth
of emotions
I follow along hoping to find my way amidst the chaos
Instead I am greeted by doubts
that clutch onto my solitude
to reveal a reality that
terrifies me

My poems are a revelation
and a cry for help
of every experience that scarred me
and every memory that still haunts me

Eyes half shut
brain racing through every rusty memory of the past
thoughts of defeat creep up
I fight the urge to give up
but my mind already gave in
to the claws of rejection

These abandoned corners of my soul
scream for attention
to be healed and sealed
like they are wound-free again

This heart is sore from holding on
to parting hope
This heart is at the end of its rope
'cause it can no longer cope
with the thought of breaking
one more time in the name of
love

I am sinking in my darkness
slowly fading into a deep black hole
a depression that is overtaking my soul

I succumb to my worries
and tell them riddles about
what my life will look like
when I no longer
go to sleep with despair

I sit with my heart and its secrets
We play tag with happiness and hope
all night long
I always lose

There is this gloomy dark space inside myself
that I never visit
for it scares and troubles me
It is a space of hollowness and loneliness
that is more terrifying than the sadness
that consumes me

To some of my abandoned dreams
I apologize for losing my battle with
depression
at your expense

I always fall for the wrong one
only to end up with a vacant heart
singing sad love songs that echo
to infinity

I am a tired soul looking for rest
in what seems the wrong places
that I often regret
I can't wait for the day
my heart and I find a shelter
to call home

I smell of burned roses
and
it echoes inside me from loneliness

If my pillow could speak
it would actually cry
for every single time
I opened up my heart
to the wrong guy

I am doing my best
but my tired soul is longing for rest
from feeling oppressed
by society's expectations that
I
truly
detest

It's like every time I grasp onto love
it slips away from me
without warning
leaving me to trace my path of loneliness
with tears of shame
without a care

I vent to the stars
and complain to the moon
about my wilted heart
and the agony it carries around
It is heavy
and pulling me to the ground

These makeshift love stories
pin me against the wall
paint my wry smile
with an even more somber color
that resembles
a slow and painful death

Everything about this very life feels temporary
The faces
The feelings
The places
The crying
The not-so-good days

I lost the sight of light to a blinding darkness
I feel defeated and close to the end
Can someone please just hold my hand?

I glimpsed my mirror
and a stranger stared back at me
Who am I now?
and
how am I supposed to carry this pain
all by myself?

In a sea of strangers
I barely recognize my heart
from all the bandages covering its flesh

How much of myself have I left
in every meaningless fairytale
every time I kissed the wrong frog?

A dissipating dream
far from this reality I created for myself
Who am I becoming?
And where am I heading with all this baggage?
I belong nowhere
floating between two seas
each catcalls me
I tease both when I want
and give in to one when I please
knowing that
I belong nowhere

Losing myself was so palpable
I could slowly feel myself
losing grip of my reality
and washing away into my chaotic brain

Have you ever cried from being so lonely
yet so many people want a spot in your life
Have you ever cried from feeling unheard
yet everyone wants to call you
Have you ever felt so empty
in a room full of people?
Have you?

"How are you?" He said
"I am crumbling and barely feeling whole
in a world that serves me halves,"
I said

How can I feel strong
in a world that sees me as a broken dove?
How can I live in a world
too casual for my intense love?
I don't know how!

When I crave normalcy
I feel the urge to get off this rollercoaster
of life
and travel back to a time when
the sun sang to flowers
and the bees danced to the beats
of my heart

What is my consolation
if after all this inevitable pain
my heart doesn't find the love
it deserves?

Tell me where I belong
torn between two cultures
one pulling me closer than the other
I used to be a desert flower
where the sun kisses the scorching sand
Fast forward to all these years
I belong to another land with no sand
a land of freedom for both women and men
where my spirit dances its cultural
boundaries away
to a newly found freedom that I cherish to this day

I am a delicate flower with prickly thorns
The side you get depends on your tone
so you can be gentle and let me bloom
or touch my thorns and endure your wounds

I hesitantly flirt with my visiting happiness
knowing it is playing me
but I have hope that
she will choose to stay
one day

I unwrinkle the receipts of deception
handed to me by different people
and write love poems on them
to read them back to myself
when my heart can't carry itself

I crack my heart open
just enough
in case I have to shut it
all over again

How does it feel to be human?
sometimes you're full of life
and sometimes you're barely alive

I am not fully broken
just chipped a little
so I will plant a rose in every crack
and turn my pain into petals

Guilt from the past
Mind trips to the future
I long to become the woman
I am destined to be
and shed the skin of whoever
I used to be

Across oceans of disappointments
I carry my heart to safety
after every lost love battle

I sail solo against the wind
to find my strength that fled
in a moment of despair and confusion

I burnt my tongue
and used my pen instead
to come to terms with my
empty
lonely and
noiseless world

Where is home?
Is it where I was born?
Or
is it where I meet people who became my own
Where is my home?

What if it was as easy to love people
as to lose them
Who would still be in our lives now?

Torn between yearning for the past
and living in the present
to get to my future safely

Thoughts fighting, blaming, and questioning each other
to comfort every doubt in my mind
Maybe not tonight
but my heart and I
will eventually get along
someday

Take me to a different world
that is kinder to my heart
that will wrap my naked soul in love
with its flaws and all

I fix my heart's posture
every time it gets tired of leaning on the wrong person
I stand tall
I stand alone
while all of my being yearns
for a gentle touch

Our breakup was the breakthrough
to finding the exact woman
I am supposed to be

It takes courage to keep an open heart
when the universe tells you not to

Graceful is this heart that wraps itself in more love
every time it gets burned
by similar fires

I am a feeler
I close my eyes
to see clearer

Please handle my heart with care
It is fragile
cracked and
almost broken

I tell my broken heart to stay strong
and not let the agony of heartbreak harden it
It has a lot more love to give

Petrichor

This seems to be a funeral
of the girl I used to be
This also is a celebration
of the woman
I fought to become

I am a wild WOMAN
returning home to herself
after wandering in the wrong places
through chaos and unanswered questions
I finally found myself
within myself

Tell the old me
I loved her so deeply
but I had to bury her
to save her from her demons
and send her away to a future
she deserves to witness

Bear with me
I am still finding my voice
blazing my own trail
and tracing my own path
to eventually live
my whole truth

It is a night like tonight
that brings darkness
to the surface of my dim light
and the silence tells my heart
stories of hope and love
of this journey called life

In my most human and vulnerable moments
I take refuge in my words
to hold me
love me
and give me back everything people took away from me

We are all hanging by a thread of hope
that seems too thin to hold
So hang on tight
'cause losing hope is losing sight
of that dim tunnel light
that we all need to win this fight
against life

I build homes of my poems
whenever my heart feels displaced
I feel home
I feel safe

There is more to all of us
than what people lay eyes on
There are hidden stories
and unspoken feelings
waiting for the right person to lean on

Undone locks of hair flirt with my face
hiding my freshly wept tears
I fake a smile to avoid answers
to questions I am familiar with
'cause I am in no hurry to lock eyes
 with what is destined for me

I weeded out the negative
people in my life
and watched my soul bloom
beautifully

This wet soil
reminds my heart
that flowers visit earth
and rainbows show off their shades
after each storm

I lay my secrets on paper
I write my wrongs
and count my sins on paper
while the world is watching

Forgiving people who hurt you
is never about them
It is about setting yourself free
from the heaviness in your heart
that can consume you alive

When all failed
I burnt my tongue
and used my pen instead
to make sense of my world

I turned my pain
into petals and
sprinkled them
all over each heart
I came
across

We often look for a sign outside of us
anywhere else
but us
when all along the sign is within us
in our gut

When life gets too dark
just remember that the sun
shows up after a long night of
darkness

You are a unique masterpiece of mistakes
so as you assemble yourself back
after each heartbreak
Enjoy your mess
Give yourself credit
and bask in your solitude

You can no longer break this heart
that has been broken
into a million pieces
and still managed to love

I learned how to color outside the lines
and call it art
in order to survive this life
that is far from what I had in mind
when I was a child

You are only too difficult to love for the wrong person
The right one will hold all your scars with both hands
and kiss your pain away

At thirty-five years old,
 I learned to explicitly say how I feel
I learned to express my likes and dislikes
I learned to never leave things unsaid for the fear of living a life
of regret
I learned that being honest with other people means being honest
with myself
And that was my getaway to freedom

Sometimes
you have to get lost
scarred
burned
and feel every emotion
in order to find your way

Like a piece of art
people will interpret you differently
Your job is to be exactly who you are
always

You master the art of living
when you extract power from
the essence of your pain

I slowly wake up to the sound of rain
keeping me company
on this very chilly morning
My sleepy face smirks
knowing I am not
alone

Raw wind graces my face through the cracks
of the window
It gently kisses my cheeks
and fills my hollow chest
with hope
that today
I will breathe fresh air
and maybe feel alive again

A glimpse of light trickles in my thoughts
I suddenly feel alive from a numbness
that I wanted to break free from for ages
I feel reborn

I grip onto my warm coffee cup
like hope for a new day ahead
As the rigid morning breeze embraces me
and welcomes my flaws far more than I do
I feel safe in its presence
I feel held even though
I am all alone

Cheers to slow mornings
and damp airy droplets
singing the morning song
to a day ahead
full of hope

As time healed my heart
I untangled myself
slowly but surely
to reveal the exact version of myself
and show up authentically
to live the life destined for me

I healed my own heart
made myself whole
and returned to myself
like a newborn

We crash
we rebuild
we move on
we heal
we are humans

To the souls wounded by defeat
from inner battles
one day
your victories will be
crowned in strength
for every time you chose
not to give up on yourself

You are here now
You are strength personified
You are new and transformed
You were made for this
long before you ever knew it

How can I ever be emotionally homeless
if home is already within myself?

Rainbow

This chapter celebrates you, WOMEN. I may or may not have met you, I may have heard of you or perhaps our paths crossed briefly, but one thing I know for sure is that I have most definitely been inspired by you. Thank you for teaching me the delicate, yet powerful balance of being a WOMAN. Your strength, resilience, and will power to show up authentically in a world that constantly tells you how to be, leaves me awestruck.

To every broken WOMAN
pick up your heart's pieces gracefully
You are more than the breakup
You are not half
You are loved
and you are
infinitely
enough

To be a WOMAN
is to be
the daughter
the wife
the sister
the friend
You give life
You are life

I told myself to
man up and suck it up
only to realize that
my strength as a WOMAN
is unmatched to that
of a man

To every immigrant WOMAN
who crossed customs at a tender age
to get her hands dirty
and build a life for herself
from the scraps of womanhood she had
I salute you

I shall not take for granted
the freedom I snatched
from the mouth of patriarchy
I shall not take for granted
the privilege to be who and what I please
while other sisters are born with destinies
handpicked for them
by others

This is a woman's body
a sanctuary
and you are only allowed to visit
if you have been blessed
by the gods of love

I am every WOMAN
I spill of greatness
and resilience
I am the WOMAN of my own dreams
I carry my heart on my sleeve
and stitch love poems on it

I am a wild WOMAN
returning home to herself
after wandering in the wrong places
through chaos and unanswered questions
I finally found myself
within myself

The earth shakes
with the sway of your hips
The moon shies away in your presence
Go ahead
show the world how to
"WOMAN"

Like honey
I drip in gold
and leak of kohl
I am an Arab WOMAN
after all

To be a WOMAN
is to move mountains
by yourself
to earn a seat at a table
made for men

Your curves are art
carved of strength
to make men weak

Your journey to womanhood is sacred
It is a celebration of every WOMAN in you
You will meet all of them
at different times
Each will
teach you
love you
and lead you
to the WOMAN
you are destined to become

How can WOMEN be so strong
yet so delicate?
Unbreakable, but crumbly?
How can they be petals and flames all at once?

Let this be our mantra
In my weakness, I am strength
In my chaos, I am strength
In my womanhood, I am strength
In my greatness, I am strength
I am a WOMAN and
I am strength

Drips of honey
between my thick thighs
mumble tales of
pride
pain
pleasure
and everything it takes to be a
WOMAN

Each month
WOMEN all over the world
drown in shame about what makes them the most "WOMEN"
They hide their tampons
to make men comfortable
They wrap pads in newspaper
to walk home from the bodega down the street
and each time I wonder:
why is the world obsessed with our flowers
Yet only want to smell them when they are "clean"?

Your curves round themselves to perfection
Your stretch marks sing lullabies proudly
You are every bit of the WOMAN you fought to become
So be her
loudly
and
unapologetically

Any man that goes after your looks
clearly lacks ambition
You are a lot of soul
sister
don't let anyone objectify you

Teach your daughters …
To love every piece of themselves
To never apologize for how they feel
Teach them to be patient with themselves
To be kind to themselves
To say no when they feel uncomfortable
about anything or around anyone
To say yes when they want to
To stand up for what they believe in
Teach them to follow their heart
Teach them to be WOMEN
whatever that means to them …

Hold your precious heart to higher standards
Protect it like you are its mother
You are a queen
and only a king deserves to savor
its love

You can be still
or wild out
You can burn it down
or build it all up
You are made of WOMAN clay
that is soft
yet difficult to mold

You are the essence of life
yet you wonder
"Am I enough?"
You are a WOMAN
resilient
and that ,sister, is a lot

Let us not make outer beauty a competition
between WOMEN
Let us make room for every woman
to show up
and shine
Let us hold each other's crown
real high

Hand in hand
we
Raise
Inspire
Support
and
Uplift each other
and that is how we
"WOMEN"
each other

To be a WOMAN
is to be a hymn of love
So pack your greatness and leave
before you beg anyone to
see your worth

Raise a glass to the WOMAN you are!
The WOMAN in you wants you to do your best
The WOMAN in you wants you to see your worth
The WOMAN in you wants you to support other WOMEN
because watching another WOMAN glow
will never dim your own light

Remember to wear your crown
and know your worth
for you are another woman's inspiration
on this earth

Within each of us
there is an outstanding WOMAN
waiting to be self-loved into existence
So please find her
honor her
and be her

You are a WOMAN
a wildflower
meant to be free
and destined to flourish
under her own conditions

You sparkle differently
when you fall in love with the WOMAN you are
and adore every detail of her being
So make sure you hold your flaws tight
and kiss them goodnight

In a world that tells us exactly how to be
we must remember
that it is okay to grow and glow
in a way that makes the most sense to us

We must lead the way
live by example
and hold the torch for the next WOMAN
lost in the darkness
so she can be the light
for the next woman
in line

Has anyone ever told you
that you radiate love
when you choose yourself?
The world needs the exact WOMAN you are
to show up for herself
Please protect your uniqueness

Whatever life throws at you
know that you will get through it
because you are not just strong
you are WOMAN strong

Lucky is the heart that
you swaddle with love
You are a gem of a
WOMAN

It is a thing of bravery
to be a WOMAN
like you

Writing is not how I see the world, it is how I feel the world.

Love and light

Amina Mejdoubi

About the author

Amina Mejdoubi is a poetess and a storyteller whose poems have been shared and enjoyed by people of all kinds. She is originally from Rabat, Morocco and currently resides in Houston, Texas where she teaches English Language Arts to ninth graders. She received her master's degree in Curriculum Instruction and Communication Arts from Wayne State College in 2009. When she is not teaching or writing poetry, Amina enjoys reading autobiographies and self development books, spending quality time with her friends, and creating content for her instagram a.m.i.n.a.m.e.j. Amina is also passionate about helping and rescuing animals and hopes that one day she can run her own non profit organization to help stray animals find homes.